ANIMAL HOMES

A TRUE BOOK

by

Ann O. Squire

Children's Press®
A Division of Scholastic Inc.

New York Toronto London Auckland Sydney
Mexico City New Delhi Hong Kong
Danbury, Connecticut

An adult and baby snail

Content Consultant
Kathy Carlstead, Ph.D.
Honolulu Zoo

Reading Consultant
Nanci R. Vargus, Ed.D.
*Primary Multiage Teacher
Decatur Township Schools,
Indianapolis, IN*

Dedication
To Emma

The photograph on the cover shows fox pups in a den. The photograph on the title page shows a wood-duck nest in a tree.

Library of Congress Cataloging-in-Publication Data

Squire, Ann O.
    Animal homes / by Ann O. Squire.
        p. cm. — (A True book)
    Includes bibliographical references (p.).
    ISBN 0-516-22189-2 (lib. bdg.)   0-516-25996-2 (pbk.)
    1. Animals—Habitations—Juvenile literature. [1. Animals—
Habitations.] I. Title. II. Series.
QL756.S68 2001
591.56'4—dc21

                                              00-057027

Contents

Some kinds of penguins build nests to protect their chicks.

Why Do Animals Need Homes?

Animals need homes for many of the same reasons that people do. What are some of those reasons? Start by thinking about your own home, and the kinds of things you do there.

Eating is one very important thing you do every day. Your

house has a kitchen where you store and prepare food. Some animals also keep food in their homes. Honeybees, for example, live in hives made up of waxy honey-combs. Each honeycomb has many six-sided cubbies, or cells, where the bees store their honey.

The cells of the honeycomb are also used as nurseries for young bees. And that may remind you of another reason

Bees store honey in some of the cells of their hive (top). Other cells are used as nurseries for bee larvae (bottom).

A fox den (right) and an alligator mound (below)

people and animals need homes. They need a safe place to raise their young. Birds' nests, alligator mounds,

Like people,
many animals
need protection
from the weather.

and the dens of polar bears
are other kinds of homes
made for raising a family.
Doesn't it feel good to
come indoors on a cold winter

day or turn up the air conditioner on a hot and humid summer night? That's another reason we need a home—to protect us from bad weather.

The desert tortoise lives in dry parts of the southwestern United States, where summer temperatures often go above 100 degrees Fahrenheit (38 degrees Celsius). To escape the heat, the tortoise digs a shallow burrow, or hole, where it can rest during the hottest part of the day.

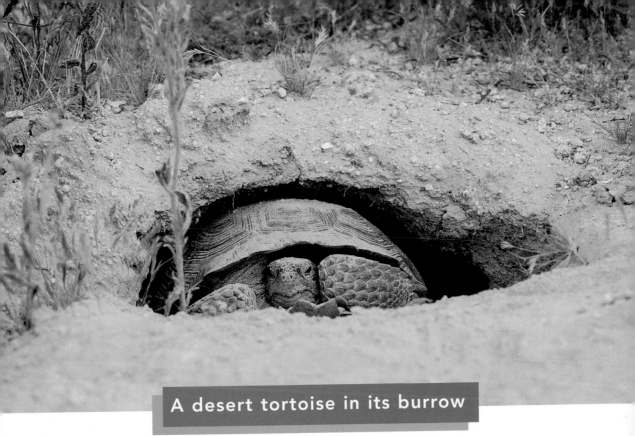

A desert tortoise in its burrow

In the winter, when temperatures fall below freezing, the tortoise digs a much deeper burrow. Then it climbs in and spends the winter there, hibernating with other tortoises.

Underground burrows also give animals a place to hide from their enemies. Prairie dogs, for example, dig long, winding burrows with many different rooms and tunnels.

A prairie dog standing near a burrow entrance

A coyote trying to invade
a prairie-dog burrow

Many peoples' homes have
a front door, a back door and
maybe even a side door. A
prairie-dog burrow has several
openings, too. If a hungry
predator invades the burrow

A spider trapping prey in its web

through the main entrance, the prairie dogs can escape out the back way.

Some animals build homes for more tricky reasons. Many spiders spin webs mainly to trap unlucky insects.

Now that you know some of the reasons animals need homes, let's find out about some unusual animal homes.

Building a Home

Many animals build their own homes. These animal architects can be birds, mammals, insects, and even fish.

The African weaverbird's name is a clue to the way this bird builds its nest. The male weaverbird gathers long blades of grass, which he

A weaverbird building its nest

knots and weaves into a sturdy ring. Then he adds grass to the ring, making a hollow ball. To keep out tree snakes, the ball is open only at the bottom.

When the nest is finished, the weaverbird calls to attract nearby females. If a female likes the nest, she moves in, and the two raise a family.

Some insects build homes, too. One of the largest and most complicated structures in the animal world is created by tiny African termites.

A termite tower may be as tall as a giraffe and contain millions of termites. The walls of the tower are made of a

rock-hard mixture of dirt and
saliva. They contain air shafts
that keep the inside of the tower
cool, even in the blazing sun.

Termite towers have many rooms.

The tower has many special rooms. It has a royal chamber, where the termite king and queen live, nurseries for the young, rooms for storing food, and even an underground garden. Most termites live for only a few years, but a termite tower may last for close to a century.

Have you ever heard people say someone is as "busy as a beaver"? You'd know what they mean if you saw how much work goes into building a beaver lodge.

First, the beavers use sticks and mud to make a dam across a stream. Then water backs up behind the dam to form a pond. In the center of the pond, the beavers build their lodge. It

Beavers use sticks (top) and mud to build a dam (middle). Then they build their lodge in the middle of the pond formed by the dam (bottom).

Beavers inside
a lodge

looks like nothing more than a pile of sticks, but the lodge has a room inside that is reached by underwater tunnels. The beavers can come and go easily, but it's almost impossible for wolves and other predators to find a way in.

Finding a Home

Bees, weaverbirds, termites, and beavers all work long and hard to build their homes. But some animals take the easy way out. They look around for ready-made lodgings.

Unlike most other crabs, the hermit crab does not have a hard shell to protect it. It

The hermit crab makes its home in an empty seashell.

needs a safe place to live, so the hermit crab searches for an empty snail shell. When it finds a shell that fits, the hermit crab squeezes inside.

It stays there until it grows too big for that shell. Then it must look for a larger shell.

The pea crab doesn't even wait until a shell is empty. This tiny crab moves in with the original owner! It squeezes into the shell of a mussel, clam, or oyster while that animal is still alive. The shellfish isn't even bothered by the pea crab sharing its home. As the shellfish filters food through its gills, the pea

A pea crab

crab catches tiny bits of food
as they float past.

The cowbird is even more
daring. Instead of building its
own nest, the female cowbird

A cowbird egg (white) in a nest containing wood thrush eggs (blue)

searches the forest for other nesting birds. When she sees a likely couple, she settles down to wait.

As soon as the unsuspecting birds leave their nest, the cowbird darts in and throws out

one of their eggs. Then she quickly lays one of her own. The nesting birds never know the difference! They raise the cowbird chick as if it were one of their own.

Burrowing Owls

Birds don't usually live underground, but one that does is the burrowing owl. These long-legged owls sometimes move into abandoned prairie-dog burrows. The birds come out in the cool of the evening to hunt small rodents, frogs, and insects.

Mobile Homes

Most people and most animals live in homes that stay in one place. But if you've ever traveled in a camper, trailer or boat, you know that some kinds of homes can move around with you. Did you know that some animals also live in "mobile homes"?

Turtles sunning themselves on a log

Tortoises and turtles move slowly. You might think they would be easy prey for any animal that wanted to eat them. But tortoises and turtles can escape into the safety of their homes in a flash, simply by pulling their head and feet inside their hard shell.

A turtle can protect itself by retreating into its shell.

Like turtles, snails can retreat into their shells.

The snail is another animal that carries its house on its back. Snails need damp conditions in order to survive. In

cold or dry weather, the snail
retreats into its spiral shell to
avoid drying out.

A kind of caterpillar called
the bagworm makes its home

A bagworm hanging from a spruce tree

out of twigs woven together with silk. The bagworm lives inside this silken case and drags its shelter along as it moves from branch to branch feeding on leaves.

Unwelcome Guests

Many animals like to live with people. Some, like dogs and cats, are pets—welcome members of the family. But others, such as cockroaches, are not so welcome.

Once cockroaches move into a person's home, it is not easy to get rid of them.

A cockroach on a plate of food

Cockroaches like dark, damp places—under the dishwasher, for example, or behind the sink. And they'll eat almost anything, including the binding on books and the glue on postage stamps. They can even live for several months without any food at all.

Larger animals may also find their way into your home. Have you heard a squeaking or rustling noise in your attic at night? It could be a squirrel

Squirrels (right) and bats (below) sometimes make their homes in people's attics.

that has found a small opening, squeezed inside, and built
a nest. Or it could be bats.
These animals, like squirrels,
can get through the tiniest
opening and move into your
house.

During the daytime, bats
sleep hanging from the rafters,
but when night falls, they head
outdoors to hunt for moths
and other flying insects.

Many other animals could
also be living in your home

Clothes moths (above) and a close-up view of a flea on a cat's ear (left)

right now. Moths munch on your woolen sweaters and blankets. Fleas suck the blood

Dust mites live in all people's homes. They are so tiny you can't even see them. This dust mite is magnified 500 times.

of your dog or your cat. And everybody's home has dust mites—tiny insects that live by the billions in bedding and carpets.

To Find Out More

Here are some additional resources to help you learn more about animal homes:

 **Books**

Robinson, W. Wright. **Animal Architects: How Mammals Build Their Amazing Homes.** Blackbirch Marketing, 1999.

Robinson, W. Wright. **Animal Architects: How Spiders and Other Silk Makers Build Their Amazing Homes.** Blackbirch Marketing, 1999.

Taylor, Barbara. **Inside Guides: Animal Homes.** DK Publishing, 1996.

Organizations and Online Sites

Animal Planet
http://www.AnimalDiscovery.com

Information on all kinds of animals, and links to nature shows on the Discovery Channel.

Habitats
http://atschool.eduweb.co.uk/sirrobhitch.suffolk/habitats/index.htm

Explores the different kinds of environments in which animals live, including ponds, deserts, rainforests, oceans, the Arctic, and many others.

National Geographic
http://www.nationalgeographic.com

Lots of interesting information on animals and nature for kids and adults.

Underdogs: Prairie Dogs at Home
http://www.nationalgeographic.com/features/98/burrow/index.html

Explore a secret world beneath the plains of North America—complex underground burrows that sprawl for miles and shelter prairie dogs from birth to death.

Important Words

abandoned deserted

architect someone who designs buildings

burrow hole or tunnel an animal makes in the ground for shelter

cell very small room or compartment

dam strong barrier or wall built across a river or stream to hold back the water

hibernate to spend the winter in a deep sleep

larvae young of certain kinds of insects

magnified made larger

nurseries places set aside for the care of babies

predator animal that captures and eats other animals

prey animal hunted by another for food

retreat to go back

saliva watery fluid from an animal's mouth

Index

Meet the Author

Ann O. Squire has a Ph.D. in animal behavior. Before becoming a writer, she studied rats, African electric fish, and other animals. Dr. Squire has written several books on animals and their behavior, including *Anteaters, Sloths, and Armadillos* and *Spiders of North America*. She lives with her children, Emma and Evan, in Bedford, New York.

Photographs ©: Animals Animals: 42 top (M. Birkhead/OSF), 40 bottom (Joe McDonald); Corbis-Bettmann: 8 top (D. Robert Franz), 38 (Robert Pickett); Peter Arnold Inc.: 4 (Fritz Polking); Photo Researchers, NY: 20 (Mark Boulton), 7 top (Scott Camazine), 7 bottom (Ken Cavanagh), 42 bottom (Stepen Dalton), 27, 29 (E.R. Degginger), 8 bottom (Stephanie Dinkins), 11 (Jerry L. Ferrara), 22 bottom (Michael Giannechini), 22 top (Bruce M. Herman), 28 (Jeff Lepore), 30 (Craig K. Lorenz), 40 top (Steven & Dave Maslowski), 43 (Oliver Meckes), 13 (Leonard Lee Rue III), 33 (David M. Schleser/Nature's Images Inc.), 34, 35 (M.H. Sharp); Stone: 32 (Kim Heacox), 2 (Kevin Summers), 17; Superstock, Inc.: 9, 14, 22 center; Tom Stack & Associates: 23 (W. Perry Conway), 1 (Joe McDonald); Tom Stack & Associates: cover (Diana L. Stratton); Visuals Unlimited: 12 (John D. Cunningham), 36 (Joe McDonald), 25 (Glenn Oliver), 19 (Kjell B. Sandued).